NOW I KNOW™

A Sunflower Grows

by MELVIN AND GILDA BERGER

SCHOLASTIC INC.

New York   Toronto   London   Auckland   Sydney
Mexico City   New Delhi   Hong Kong   Buenos Aires

What flower looks like the sun?

A sunflower!

There are many different kinds of sunflowers.

DID YOU KNOW?
The sunflower center is called the head.

The big round center is like the sun.

The bright yellow petals look like the rays of the sun.

Hundreds of tiny flowers
make up the center.

Each tiny flower will become
a sunflower seed.

Plants grow from seeds.

Sunflowers grow from sunflower seeds.

In spring, you can plant
the sunflower seeds.

The seeds are planted in soil.

The seeds start to grow.

The stems grow up.
The roots grow down.

Soon you see a green shoot.

DID YOU KNOW? Sunflower plants have big, heart-shaped leaves.

More leaves grow on the stem.

Do you see the bud?
What's inside?

ZOOM!

A young sunflower!

ZOOM!

Sunflowers
need water.

Sunflowers need sun.

The open flowers face the sun.

They attract birds, bees,
and butterflies.

DID YOU KNOW? Sunflower plants dry up in the fall.

Look at the sunflowers now.

The seeds are ready.

Farmers pick the dry sunflowers.

They collect the seeds.

Sunflower seeds are good to eat.

They can also be pressed to
make sunflower oil.

Many seeds fall to the ground.

Each seed may grow up
to be a new sunflower!

GLOSSARY

Bud: the part of the plant that grows into a leaf or flower.

Flower: The part of a plant that makes seeds or fruit.

Head: The round center of a sunflower.

Leaves: The flat green parts of plants that grow out of stems.

Petal: The colored outer part of a flower.

Plant: A living thing usually with stems, roots, and leaves.

Pressed: Squeezed hard.

Rays: Narrow beams of light.

Root: The part of a plant that grows under the ground.

Seed: The part of a plant from which new plants can grow.

Shoot: A young plant that has just appeared above the ground.

Soil: Dirt or earth in which plants grow.

Stem: The part of a plant from which the leaves and flowers grow.

Sun: The star that gives us light and warmth.